AF527544

**James Allen** (November 28, 1864–1912) was a British philosophical writer known for his inspirational books and poetry and as a pioneer of the self-help movement. His best known work, *As a Man Thinketh*, has been mass produced since its publication in 1903. It has been a source of inspiration to motivational and self-help authors.

Born in Leicester, England, into a working-class family, Allen was the eldest of two brothers. His mother could neither read nor write while his father, William, was a factory knitter. In 1879, following a downturn in the textile trade of Central England, Allen's father travelled alone to America to find work and establish a new home for the family. Within two days of arriving, his father was pronounced dead at New York City Hospital, in what was believed to be a case of robbery and murder. At age fifteen, with the family now facing economic disaster, Allen was forced to leave school and find work.

For much of the 1890s, Allen worked as a private secretary and stationer in several British manufacturing firms. In 1893, Allen moved to London where he met Lily Louisa Oram who he then wed in 1895. In 1898, Allen found an occupation in which he could showcase his spiritual and social interests as a writer for the magazine *The Herald of the Golden Age.* At this time, Allen entered a creative period where he then published his first book of many books, *From Poverty to Power* (1901). In 1902, Allen began to publish his own spiritual magazine, *The Light of Reason*, later retitled *The Epoch.*

In 1903, Allen published his third and most famous book, *As a Man Thinketh.* Loosely based on the biblical proverb, "As a man thinketh in his heart, so is he," the small work eventually became read around the world and brought Allen posthumous fame as one of the pioneering figures of modern inspirational thought. The book's minor audience allowed Allen to quit his secretarial work and pursue his writing and editing career. In 1903, the Allen family retired to the town of Ilfracombe where Allen would spend the rest of his life. Continuing to publish *The Epoch*, Allen produced 19 works in the following nine years, until his death in 1912.

Following his death in 1912, his wife continued publishing the magazine under the name *The Epoch.* Lily Allen summarised her husband's literary mission in the preface to one of his posthumously published manuscripts, *Foundation Stones to Happiness and Success*, saying: "He never wrote theories, or for the sake of writing, but he wrote when he had a message, and it became a message only when he had lived it out in his own life, and knew that it was good. Thus he wrote facts, which he had proven by practice."

# *As a Man Thinketh*

JAMES ALLEN

**Om Books International**

Reprinted in 2020 by

**Om Books International**

**Corporate & Editorial Office**
A-12, Sector 64, Noida 201 301
Uttar Pradesh, India
Phone: +91 120 477 4100
Email: editorial@ombooks.com
Website: www.ombooksinternational.com

**Sales Office**
107, Ansari Road, Darya Ganj,
New Delhi 110 002, India
Phone: +91 11 4000 9000
Fax: +91 11 2327 8091
Email: sales@ombooks.com
Website: www.ombooks.com

This edition copyright © Om Books International 2016

ALL RIGHTS RESERVED. No part of this book may be reproduced or transmitted in any form by any means, electronic or mechanical, including photocopying and recording, or by any information storage and retrieval system, except as may be expressly permitted in writing by the publisher.

ISBN: 978-93-85609-77-0

Printed in India

10 9 8 7 6 5 4 3

*Mind is the Master power that moulds and makes,*
*And Man is Mind, and evermore he takes*
*The tool of Thought, and shaping what he wills,*
*Brings forth a thousand joys, a thousand ills:*
*He thinks in secret, and it comes to pass—*
*Environment (World) is but his looking-glass.*

# Contents

*Whatever you can do, or dream you can, begin it—*
*Boldness has genius, power, and magic in it.*

—Goethe

# Foreword

I looked around upon the world, and saw that it was shadowed by sorrow and scorched by the fierce fires of suffering. And I looked for the cause. I looked around, but I could not find it; I looked in books, but I could not find it; I looked within, and found there both the cause and the self-made nature of that cause. I looked again, and deeper, and found the remedy. I found one Law, the Law of love; one life, the life of adjustment to that Law; one Truth, the Truth of a conquered mind and a quiet and obedient heart.

And I dreamed of writing books which would help men and women, whether rich or poor, learned or unlearned, worldly or unworldly to find within themselves the source of all success, all happiness, all accomplishment, all truth. And the dream remained with me, and at last became substantial; and now I send forth these books into the world on a misson of healing and blessedness, knowing that they cannot fail to reach the homes and hearts of those who are waiting and ready to receive them.

James Allen
Broad Park Avenue
Ilfracombe
England

# 1

# THOUGHT AND CHARACTER

*As a being of power, intelligence, and love and the lord of his own thoughts, man holds the key to every situation, and contains within himself that transforming and regenerative agency by which he makes himself what he wills.*

# Thought and Character

The aphorism, "As a man thinketh in his heart so is he," not only embraces the whole of a man's being, but is so comprehensive that it reaches out to every condition and circumstance of his life. A man is literally what he thinks, his character being the complete sum of all his thoughts.

As the plant springs from, and could not be without the seed, so every act of a man springs from the hidden seeds of thought, and could not have appeared without them. This applies equally to those acts called "spontaneous" and "unpremeditated" as to those, which are deliberately executed.

An act is the blossom of thought, and joy and suffering are its fruits; thus does a man garner in the sweet and bitter fruitage of his own husbandry.

*Thought in the mind*

*hath made us what we are.*

*By thought was wrought and built*

*If a man's mind*

*has evil thoughts,*

*pain comes on him*

*as comes the wheel behind the ox...*

*If one endures in purity of thought,*

*joy follows him*

*as his own shadow—sure.*

Man is a growth by law, and not a creation by artifice, and cause-and-effect is as absolute and undeviating in the hidden realm of thought as in the world of visible and material things.

A noble and God-like character is not a thing of favour or chance, but is the natural result of continued effort in right thinking, the effect of long-cherished association with God-like thoughts. An ignoble and bestial character, by the same process, is the result of the continued harbouring of grovelling thoughts.

## You are the Master of Your Fate

Man is made or unmade by himself; in the armoury of thought he forges the weapons by which he destroys himself; he also fashions the tools with which he builds for himself heavenly mansions of joy and strength and peace. By the right choice and true application of thought, man ascends to the Divine perfection; by the abuse and wrong application of thought, he descends below the level of the beast. Between these two extremes are all the grades of character, and man is their maker and master.

Of all the beautiful truths pertaining to the soul which have been restored and brought to light in this age, none is more gladdening or fruitful of Divine promise and confidence than this—that man is the master of thought, the moulder of character, and the maker and shaper of condition, environment, and destiny.

As a being of power, intelligence, and love, and the lord of his own thoughts, man holds the key to every situation, and contains within himself that transforming and regenerative agency by which he may make himself what he wills.

Man is always the master, even in his weaker and most abandoned state; but in his weakness and degradation, he is the foolish master who misgoverns his "household". When he begins to reflect upon his condition, and to search diligently for the Law upon which his being is established, he then becomes the wise master, directing his energies with intelligence, and fashioning his thoughts to fruitful issues.

Such is the conscious master, and man can only thus become by discovering within himself the laws of thought; which discovery is totally a matter of application, self-analysis, and experience.

## Seek and You shall Find

Only by much searching and mining, are gold and diamonds obtained, and man can find every truth connected with his being, if he will dig deep into the mine of his soul.

Man is the maker of his character, the moulder of his life, and the builder of his destiny. This he may prove unerringly, if he will watch, control, and alter his thoughts, tracing their effects upon himself, upon others, and upon his life and circumstances; this he may prove by linking cause and effect by patient practice and investigation, and utilising his every experience, even to the most trivial, everyday occurrence, as a means of obtaining that knowledge of himself which is understanding, wisdom and power.

In this direction, as in no other, is the law absolute that "He that seeketh findeth; and to him that knocketh, it shall be opened"; for only by patience, practice, and ceaseless importunity can a man enter the door of the Temple of Knowledge.

# 2

# EFFECT OF THOUGHT ON CIRCUMSTANCES

*The human will, that force unseen,*
*the offspring of a deathless soul,*
*can hew a way to any goal,*
*though walls of granite intervene.*

# Effect of Thought on Circumstances

Man's mind may be likened to a garden, which may be intelligently cultivated or allowed to run wild; but whether cultivated or neglected, it must, and will, bring forth. If no useful seeds are put into it, then an abundance of useless weed-seeds will fall therein, and will continue to produce their kind.

Just as a gardener cultivates his plot, keeping it free from weeds, and growing the flowers and fruits which he requires, so may a man tend the garden of his mind, weeding out all the wrong, useless, and impure thoughts, and cultivating towards perfection, the flowers and fruits of right, useful, and pure thoughts.

By pursuing this process, a man sooner or later discovers that he is the master-gardener of his soul, the director of his life. He also reveals, within himself, the laws of thought, and understands, with ever-increasing accuracy, how the thought forces and mind elements operate in the shaping of his character, circumstances, and destiny.

Thought and character are one, and as character can only manifest and discover itself through environment and circumstance, the outer conditions of a person's life will always be found to be harmoniously related to his inner state. This does not mean that a man's circumstances at any given time, are an indication of his entire character, but that those circumstances are so intimately connected with some vital thought-element within himself that, for the time being, they are indispensable to his development.

Every man is where he is by the law of his beings; the thoughts which he has built into his character have brought him there, and in the arrangement of his life there is no element of chance.

All is the result of a law which cannot err. This is just as true of those who feel "out of harmony" with their surroundings as of those who are contented with them.

## Circumstances Grow Out of Thoughts

As a progressive and evolving being, man is where he is that he may learn; that he may grow; and as he learns the spiritual lesson which any circumstance contains for him, it passes away and gives place to other circumstances.

Man is buffeted by circumstances so long as he believes himself to be the creature of outside conditions. But when he realises that he is a creative power, and that he may command the hidden soil and seeds of his being out of which circumstances grow, he then becomes the rightful master of himself.

That circumstances grow out of thought, every man knows who has for any length of time practised self-control and self-purification, for he will have noticed that the alteration in his circumstances has been in exact ratio with his altered mental condition. So true is this that when a man earnestly applies himself to remedy the defects in his character, and makes swift and marked progress, he passes rapidly through a succession of vicissitudes.

The soul attracts that which it secretly harbours, that which it loves, and also that which it fears; it reaches the height of its cherished aspirations; it falls to the level of its unchastened desires—and circumstances are the means by which the soul receives its own.

Every thought-seed sown or allowed to fall into the mind, and to take root there, produces its own, blossoming sooner or later into act, and bearing its own fruitage (fruits) of opportunity and circumstance. Good thoughts bear good fruit; bad thoughts bad fruit.

The outer world of circumstance shapes itself to the inner world of thought, and both pleasant and unpleasant external conditions are factors, which make for the ultimate good of the individual. As the reaper of his own harvest, man learns both by suffering and bliss.

Following the innermost desires, aspirations, thoughts, by which he allows himself to be dominated (pursuing the will-o'-the-wisps of impure imaginings or steadfastly walking the highway of strong and high endeavour), a man at last arrives at their fruition and fulfilment in the outer conditions of his life. The laws of growth and adjustment are everywhere in effect.

## Justice is Exact

A man does not come to the almshouse or the jail by the tyranny of fate or circumstance, but by the pathway of grovelling (low) thoughts and base desires. Nor does a pure-minded man fall suddenly into crime by stress of any mere external force; the criminal thought had long been secretly fostered in the heart, and the hour of opportunity revealed its gathered power. Circumstance does not make the man; it reveals him to himself. No such conditions can exist as descending into vice and its attendant sufferings apart from vicious inclinations, or ascending into virtue and its pure happiness without the continued cultivation of virtuous aspirations. Man, therefore, as the lord and master of thought, is the maker of himself, the shaper and author of environment.

Even at birth, the soul comes to its own and through every step of its earthly pilgrimage it attracts those combinations of conditions which reveal itself, which are the reflections of its own purity and, impurity, its strength and weakness.

Men do not attract that which they want, but that which they are. Their whims, fancies, and ambitions are thwarted at every step, but their inmost thoughts and desires are fed with their own food, be it foul or clean. The "divinity that shapes our ends" is in ourselves; it is our very self. Man is manacled (imprisoned) only by himself. Thought and action are the jailers of Fate—they imprison, being base; they are also the angels of Freedom—they liberate, being noble. Not what he wishes and prays for does a man get, but what he justly earns. His wishes and prayers are only gratified and answered when they harmonise with his thoughts and actions.

In the light of this truth, what, then, is the meaning of "fighting against circumstances"? It means that a man is continually revolting against an effect without, while all the time he is nourishing and preserving its cause in his heart. That cause may take the form of a conscious vice or an unconscious weakness; but whatever it is, it stubbornly retards the efforts of its possessor, and thus calls aloud for remedy.

## Three Examples of Ignorance

Men are anxious to improve their circumstances, but are unwilling to improve themselves; they therefore remain bound. The man who does not shrink from self-crucifixion can never fail to accomplish the object upon which his heart is set. This is as true of earthly as of heavenly things. Even the man whose sole object is to acquire wealth must be prepared to make great personal sacrifices before he can accomplish his object; and how much more so he who would realise a strong and well-poised life?

Here is a man who is wretchedly poor. He is extremely anxious that his surroundings and home comforts should be improved, yet all the time he shirks his work, and considers he is justified in trying to deceive his employer on the ground of the insufficiency of his wages. Such a man does not understand the simplest rudiments of those principles which are the basis of true prosperity. He is not only totally unfitted to rise out of his wretchedness, but is actually attracting to himself a still deeper wretchedness by dwelling in, and acting out indolent, deceptive, and unmanly thoughts.

Here is a rich man who is the victim of a painful and persistent disease as the result of gluttony. He is willing to give large sums of money to get rid of it, but he will not sacrifice his gluttonous desires. He wants to gratify his taste for rich and unnatural foods and have his health as well. Such a man is totally unfit to have health, because he has not yet learned the first principles of a healthy life.

Here is an employer of labour who adopts crooked measures to avoid paying the regulation (fair) wage, and, in the hope of making larger profits, reduces the wages of his work people. Such a man is altogether unfitted for prosperity, and when he finds himself bankrupt, both as regards to reputation and riches, he blames circumstances, not knowing that he is the sole author of his condition.

I have introduced these three cases merely as illustrative of the truth that man is the cause (though nearly always is unconsciously) of his circumstances, and that, whilst aiming at a good end, he is continually frustrating its accomplishment by encouraging thoughts and desires which cannot possibly harmonise with that end. Such cases could be multiplied and varied almost indefinitely, but this is not necessary, as the reader can, if he so resolves, trace the action of the laws of thought in his own mind and life, and until this is done, mere external facts cannot serve as a ground of reasoning.

## Good Cannot Produce Evil

Circumstances, however, are so complicated, thought is so deeply rooted, and the conditions of happiness vary so vastly with individuals, that a man's entire soul-condition (although it may be known to himself) cannot be judged by another from the external aspect of his life alone. A man may be honest in certain directions, yet suffer privations; a man may be dishonest in certain directions, yet acquire wealth.

The conclusion usually formed that the one man fails because of his particular honesty, and that the other prospers because of his particular dishonesty, is the result of a superficial judgment, which assumes that the dishonest man is almost totally corrupt, and the honest man almost entirely virtuous. In the light of a deeper knowledge and wider experience, such judgment is found to be erroneous.

The dishonest man may have some admirable virtues, which the other does not possess; and the honest man obnoxious vices which are absent in the other. The honest man reaps the good results of his honest thoughts and acts; he also brings upon himself the sufferings, which his vices produce. The dishonest man likewise harvests his own suffering and happiness.

It is pleasing to human vanity to believe one suffers because of one's virtue; but not until man has rooted out every sickly, bitter and impure thought from his mind, and washed every sinful stain from his soul, can he be in a position to know and declare that his sufferings are the result of his good, and not of his bad qualities.

And on the way to, yet long before he has reached, that supreme perfection, he will have found, working in his mind and life, the Great Law which is absolutely just, and which cannot, therefore, give good for evil, evil for good. Possessed of such knowledge, he will then know, looking back upon his past ignorance and blindness, that his life is, and always was, justly ordered, and that all his past experiences, good and bad, were the equitable outworking of his evolving, yet unevolved self.

## You are What You Think

Good thoughts and actions can never produce bad results; bad thoughts and actions can never produce good results. This is but saying that nothing can come from corn but corn, nothing from nettles but nettles. Men understand this law in the natural world, and work with it; but few understand it in the mental and moral world (though its operation there is just as simple and undeviating), and they, therefore, do not co-operate with it.

Suffering is always the effect of wrong thought in some direction. It is an indication that the individual is out of harmony with himself, with the law of his being. The sole and supreme use of suffering is to purify, to burn out all that is useless and impure. Suffering ceases for him who is pure. There could be no object in burning gold after the dross had been removed, and a perfectly pure and enlightened being could not suffer.

The circumstances, which a man encounters with suffering, are the result of his own mental disharmony. The circumstances which a man encounters with blessedness, are the result of his own mental harmony. Blessedness, not material possessions, is the measure of right thought; wretchedness, not lack of material possessions, is the measure of wrong thought. A man may be cursed and rich; he may be blessed and poor. Blessedness and riches are only joined together when the riches are rightly and wisely used; and the poor man only descends into wretchedness when he regards his lot as a burden unjustly imposed.

Lack and excess are the two extremes of wretchedness. They are both equally unnatural and the result of mental disorder. A man is not rightly conditioned until he is a happy, healthy, and prosperous being; and happiness, health, and prosperity are the result of a harmonious adjustment of the inner with the outer, of the man with his surroundings.

## Discover the Hidden Powers Within

A man only begins to be a man when he ceases to whine and revile, and commences to search for the hidden justice which regulates his life. And as he adapts his mind to that regulating factor, he ceases to accuse others as the cause of his condition, and builds himself up in strong and noble thoughts; ceases to kick against circumstances, but begins to use them as aids to his more rapid progress, and as a means of discovering the hidden powers and possibilities within himself.

Law, not confusion, is the dominating principle of the universe. Justice, not injustice, is the soul and substance of life. And righteousness, not corruption, is the moulding and moving force in the spiritual government of the world. This being so, man has but to right himself to find that the universe is right; and during the process of putting himself right, he will find that as he alters his thoughts towards things and other people, things and other people will alter towards him.

The proof of this truth is in every person, and it therefore admits of easy investigation by systematic introspection and self-analysis. Let a man radically alter his thoughts, and he will be astonished at the rapid transformation it will effect in the material conditions of his life.

## The Aftermath of Corrupt Thoughts

Men imagine that thought can be kept secret, but it cannot; it rapidly crystallises into habit, and habit solidifies into circumstance.

- Bestial thoughts crystallise into habits of drunkenness and sensuality, which solidify into circumstances of destitution and disease.
- Impure thoughts of every kind crystallise into enervating and confusing habits, which solidify into distracting and adverse circumstances.
- Thoughts of fear, doubt, and indecision crystallise into weak, unmanly, and irresolute habits, which solidify into circumstances of failure, indigence and slavish dependence.
- Lazy thoughts crystallise into habits of uncleanliness and dishonesty, which solidify into circumstances of foulness and beggary (poverty).
- Hateful and condemnatory thoughts crystallise into habits of accusation and

violence, which solidify into circumstances of injury and persecution.

- Selfish thoughts of all kinds crystallise into habits of self-seeking, which solidify into circumstances more or less distressing.

## The Aftermath of Beautiful Thoughts

On the other hand, beautiful thoughts of all kinds crystallise into habits of grace and kindliness, which solidify into friendly and sunny circumstances:

- Pure thoughts crystallise into habits of temperance and self-control, which solidify into circumstances of repose and peace.
- Thoughts of courage, self-reliance, and decision crystallise into manly (strong) habits, which solidify into circumstances of success, plenty, and freedom.
- Energetic thoughts crystallise into habits of cleanliness and industry, which solidify into circumstances of pleasantness and peace.
- Gentle and forgiving thoughts crystallise into habits of gentleness, which solidify

into protective and preservative (safe and health) circumstances.

- Loving and unselfish thoughts crystallise into habits of self-forgetfulness for others, which solidify into circumstances of sure and abiding prosperity and true riches.

## Thoughts Shape Your Circumstances

A particular train of thought persisted in, be it good or bad, cannot fail to produce its results on the character and circumstances. A man cannot directly choose his circumstances, but he can choose his thoughts, and so indirectly, yet surely, shape his circumstances.

Nature helps every man to the gratification of the thoughts, which he most encourages, and opportunities are presented which will most speedily bring to the surface both the good and evil thoughts.

Let a man cease from his sinful (negative and destructive) thoughts, and all the world will soften towards him, and be ready to help him; let him put away his weakly and sickly thoughts, and lo! opportunities will spring up on every hand to aid his strong resolves. Let him encourage good thoughts, and no hard fate shall bind him down to wretchedness (misery) and shame.

The world is your kaleidoscope, and the varying combinations of colours, which at every succeeding moment it presents to you are the exquisitely adjusted pictures of your ever-moving thoughts.

*So you will be what you will to be.*
*Let failure find its false content*
*in that poor word, 'environment',*
*but spirit scorns it, and is free.*

*It masters time, it conquers space;*
*it cows that boastful trickster, Chance,*
*and bids the tyrant Circumstance*
*uncrown, and fill a servant's place.*

*The human will, that force unseen,*
*the offspring of a deathless soul,*
*can hew a way to any goal,*
*though walls of granite intervene.*

*Be not impatient in delays*
*but wait as one who understands;*
*when spirit rises and commands*
*the gods are ready to obey.*

# 3

# EFFECT OF THOUGHT ON HEALTH AND THE BODY

*The body is a delicate and plastic instrument, and responds readily to the thoughts by which it is impressed, and habits of thought will produce their own effects, good or bad, upon it.*

# Effect of Thought on Health and the Body

The body is the servant of the mind. It obeys the operations of the mind, whether they be deliberately chosen or automatically expressed. At the bidding of unlawful (unhealthy) thoughts, the body sinks rapidly into disease and decay; at the command of glad and beautiful thoughts, it becomes clothed with youthfulness and beauty.

Disease and health, like circumstances, are rooted in thought. Sickly thoughts will express themselves through a sickly body. Thoughts of fear have been known to kill a man as speedily as a bullet, and they are continually killing thousands of people just as surely, though less rapidly. The people who live in fear of disease are the people who get it. Anxiety quickly demoralises the whole body, and lays it open to the entrance of disease; while impure thoughts, even if not physically indulged, will soon shatter the nervous system.

Strong, pure, and happy thoughts build up the body in vigour and grace. The body is a delicate and plastic instrument, which responds readily to the thoughts by which it is impressed, and habits of thought will produce their own effects, good or bad, upon it.

Men will continue to have impure and poisoned blood, so long as they propagate unclean thoughts. Out of a clean heart comes a clean life and a clean body. Out of a defiled mind proceeds a defiled life and a corrupt body. Thought is the fountain of action, life, and manifestation; make the fountain (source) pure, and all will be pure.

Change of diet will not help a man who will not change his thoughts. When a man makes his thoughts pure, he no longer desires impure food.

Clean thoughts make clean habits. The so-called saint who does not wash his body is not a saint. He, who has strengthened and purified his thoughts, does not need to consider the malevolent microbe.

## Your Mind Determines Your Health

If you would protect your body, guard your mind. If you would renew your body, beautify your mind. Thoughts of malice, envy, disappointment, despondency, rob the body of its health and grace. A sour face does not come by chance; it is made by sour thoughts. Wrinkles that mar are drawn by folly, passion, and pride.

I know a woman of ninety-six who has the bright, innocent face of a girl. I know a man well under middle age whose face is drawn into inharmonious contours. The one is the result of a sweet and sunny disposition; the other is the outcome of passion and discontent.

As you cannot have a sweet and wholesome abode (home) unless you admit the air and sunshine freely into your rooms, so a strong body and a bright, happy, or serene countenance (face) can only result from the free admittance into the mind of thoughts of joy and goodwill and serenity.

On the faces of the aged there are wrinkles made by sympathy; others wrought by strong and pure thought; and others are carved by passion:

who cannot distinguish them? With those who have lived righteously, age is calm, peaceful, and softly mellowed, like the setting sun. I have recently seen a philosopher on his deathbed. He was not old except in years. He died as sweetly and peacefully as he had lived.

There is no physician like a cheerful thought for dissipating the ills of the body; there is no comforter to compare with goodwill for dispersing the shadows of grief and sorrow. To live continually in thoughts of ill-will, cynicism, suspicion, and envy, is to be confined in a self-made prison-hole. But to think well of all, to be cheerful with all, to patiently learn to find the good in all—such unselfish thoughts are the very portals of heaven; and to dwell day by day in thoughts of peace towards every creature will bring abounding peace to their possessor.

# 4

# THOUGHT AND PURPOSE

*He who has conquered doubt and fear has conquered failure. His every thought is allied with power; and all difficulties are bravely met and wisely overcome.*

# Thought and Purpose

Until thought is linked with purpose, there is no intelligent accomplishment. With the majority the ship of thought is allowed to "drift" upon the ocean of life. Aimlessness is a common vice, and such drifting must not continue for him who would steer clear of catastrophe and destruction.

They who have no central purpose in their life fall an easy prey to petty worries, fears, troubles, and self-pityings, all of which are indications of weakness, which lead, just as surely as deliberately planned sins (though by a different route), to failure, unhappiness, and loss, for weakness cannot persist in a power evolving universe.

A man should conceive of a legitimate purpose in his heart, and set out to accomplish it. He should make this purpose the centralising point of his thoughts. It may take the form of a spiritual ideal, or it may be a worldly object, according to his nature for the time being; but whatever it is, he should steadily focus his thought-forces upon the object, which he has set before him.

He should make this purpose his supreme duty, and should devote himself to its attainment, not allowing his thoughts to wander away into ephemeral (short-lived) fancies, longings, and imaginings. This is the royal road to self-control and true concentration of thought.

Even if he fails again and again to accomplish his purpose (as he necessarily must until weakness is overcome), the strength of character gained will be the measure of his true success, and this will form a new starting point for future power and triumph.

Those who are not prepared for the apprehension of a great purpose should fix the thoughts upon the faultless performance of their duty, no matter how insignificant their task may appear. Only in this way can the thoughts be gathered and focussed, and resolution and energy be developed, which being done, there is nothing which may not be accomplished.

## Strength Grows with Purpose

The weakest soul, knowing its own weakness, and believing this truth that strength can only be developed by effort and practice, will, thus believing, at once begin to exert itself. And by adding effort to effort, patience to patience, and strength to strength, will never cease to develop, and will at last grow divinely strong.

As the physically weak man can make himself strong by careful and patient training, so the man of weak thoughts can make them strong by exercising himself in right thinking.

To put away aimlessness and weakness, and to begin to think with purpose, is to enter the ranks of those strong ones who only recognise failure as one of the pathways to attainment; who make all conditions serve them; and who think strongly, attempt fearlessly, and accomplish masterfully.

Having conceived of his purpose, a man should mentally mark out a straight pathway to its achievement, looking neither to the right nor the left. Doubts and fears should be rigorously excluded. They are disintegrating elements, which break up the straight line of effort, rendering it crooked, ineffectual and useless. Thoughts of doubt and fear never accomplished anything, and never can. They always lead to failure. Purpose, energy, power to do, and all strong thoughts cease when doubt and fear creep in.

## Eliminate Doubt and Fear

The will to do springs from the knowledge that we can do. Doubt and fear are the great enemies of knowledge, and he who encourages them, who does not slay them, thwarts himself at every step.

He who has conquered doubt and fear has conquered failure. His every thought is allied with power, and all difficulties are bravely met and wisely overcome. His purposes are seasonably planted, and they bloom and bring forth fruit, which does not fall prematurely to the ground.

Thought allied fearlessly to purpose becomes creative force. He who knows this is ready to become something higher and stronger than a mere bundle of wavering thoughts and fluctuating sensations; he who does this—align his thoughts fearlessly with his purpose—has become the conscious and intelligent wielder of his mental powers.

# 5

# THE THOUGHT-FACTOR IN ACHIEVEMENT

*All achievements, whether in the business, intellectual, or spiritual world, are the result of definitely directed thoughts, are governed by the same law, and are of the same method; the only difference lies in the object of attainment.*

# The Thought-Factor in Achievement

All that a man achieves and all that he fails to achieve is the direct result of his own thoughts. In a justly ordered universe, where loss of equipoise (equilibrium) would mean total destruction, individual responsibility must be absolute. A man's weakness and strength, purity and impurity, are his own, and not another man's. They are brought about by himself, and not by another; and they can only be altered by himself, never by another. His condition is also his own, and not another man's. His suffering and his happiness are evolved from within. As he thinks, so he is; as he continues to think, so he remains.

A strong man cannot help a weaker unless that weaker is willing to be helped, and even then, the weak man must become strong of himself;

he must, by his own efforts, develop the strength which he admires in another. None but himself can alter his condition.

It has been usual for men to think and to say, "Many men are slaves because one is an oppressor; let us hate the oppressor." Now, however, there is amongst an increasing few a tendency to reverse this judgment, and to say, "One man is an oppressor because many are slaves; let us despise the slaves."

The truth is that oppressor and slave (oppressed) are co-operators in ignorance, and, while seeming to afflict each other, are in reality afflicting themselves. A perfect knowledge perceives the action of law in the weakness of the oppressed and the misapplied power of the oppressor; a perfect love, seeing the suffering, which both states entail, condemns neither; a perfect compassion embraces both oppressor and oppressed.

He who has conquered weakness, and has put away all selfish thoughts, belongs neither to oppressor nor oppressed. He is free.

A man can only rise, conquer, and achieve by lifting up his thoughts. He can only remain weak, and abject, and miserable, by refusing to lift up his thoughts.

## There is No Progress Without Sacrifice

Before a man can achieve anything, even in worldly things, he must lift his thoughts above slavish (extreme self-indulgence) animal indulgence. He may not, in order to succeed, give up all animality and selfishness, by any means; but a portion of it must, at least, be sacrificed.

A man whose first thought is bestial indulgence could neither think clearly nor plan methodically; he could not find and develop his latent resources, and would fail in any undertaking. Not having commenced to manfully (effectively) control his thoughts, he is not in a position to control affairs and to adopt serious responsibilities. He is not fit to act independently and stand alone. But he is limited only by the thoughts, which he chooses.

There can be no progress, no achievement without sacrifice, and a man's worldly success will be in the measure that he sacrifices his confused animal thoughts, and fixes his mind on the development of his plans, and the strengthening of his resolution and self-reliance. And the higher he lifts his thoughts, the more manly, upright and righteous he becomes, the greater will be his success, the more blessed and enduring will be his achievements.

The universe does not favour the greedy, the dishonest, the vicious, although on the mere surface it may sometimes appear to do so; it helps the honest, the magnanimous, the virtuous. All the great teachers of the ages have declared this in varying forms, and to prove and know it a man has but to persist in making himself more and more virtuous by lifting up his thoughts.

## You Rise or Fall by Your Thoughts

Intellectual achievements are the result of thought consecrated to the search for knowledge, or for the beautiful and true in life and nature. Such achievements may be sometimes connected with vanity and ambition, but they are not the outcome of those characteristics; they are the natural outgrowth of long and arduous effort, and of pure and unselfish thoughts.

Spiritual achievements are the consummation of holy aspirations. He who lives constantly in the conception of noble and lofty thoughts, who dwells upon all that is pure and unselfish, will, as surely as the sun reach its zenith and the moon its full, become wise and noble in character, and rise into a position of influence and blessedness.

Achievement, of whatever kind, is the crown of effort, the diadem of thought. By the aid of self-control, resolution, purity, righteousness, and well-directed thought a man ascends; by the aid of animality, indolence, impurity, corruption, and confusion of thought a man descends.

A man may rise to high success in the world, and even to lofty altitudes in the spiritual realm, and again descend into weakness and wretchedness by allowing arrogant, selfish, and corrupt thoughts to take possession of him.

Victories attained by right thought can only be maintained by watchfulness. Many give way when success is assured, and rapidly fall back into failure.

All achievements, whether in the business, intellectual, or spiritual world, are the result of definitely directed thought, are governed by the same law and are of the same method; the only difference lies in the object of attainment.

He who would accomplish little must sacrifice little; he who would achieve much must sacrifice much; he who would attain highly must sacrifice greatly.

# 6

# VISIONS AND IDEALS

*He who cherishes a beautiful vision,*
*a lofty ideal in his heart,*
*will one day realise it...*
*Dream lofty dreams, and as you dream,*
*so shall you become.*

# Visions and Ideals

The dreamers are the saviours of the world. As the visible world is sustained by the invisible, so men, through all their trials and sins and sordid vocations (mistakes and sufferings), are nourished by the beautiful visions of their solitary dreamers. Humanity cannot forget its dreamers; it cannot let their ideals fade and die; it lives in them; it knows them as the realities which it shall one day see and know.

Composer, sculptor, painter, poet, prophet, sage, these are the makers of the after-world, the architects of heaven. The world is beautiful because they have lived; without them, labouring humanity would perish.

He who cherishes a beautiful vision, a lofty ideal in his heart, will one day realise it. Columbus cherished a vision of another world, and he discovered it; Copernicus fostered the vision of a multiplicity of worlds and a wider universe, and he revealed it; Buddha beheld the vision of a spiritual world of stainless beauty and perfect peace, and he entered into it.

Cherish your visions; cherish your ideals; cherish the music that stirs in your heart, the beauty that forms in your mind, the loveliness that drapes your purest thoughts, for out of them will grow all delightful conditions, all heavenly environment; of these; if you but remain true to them, your world will at last be built.

To desire is to obtain; to aspire is to achieve. Shall man's basest desires receive the fullest measure of gratification, and his purest aspirations starve for lack of sustenance? Such is not the law: such a condition of things can never obtain: "Ask and receive".

Dream lofty dreams, and as you dream, so shall you become. Your vision is the promise of what you shall one day be; your ideal is the prophecy of what you shall at last unveil.

## Dreams Beget Realities

The greatest achievement was at first and for a time a dream. The oak sleeps in the acorn; the bird waits in the egg; and in the highest vision of the soul, a waking angel stirs. Dreams are the seedlings of realities.

Your circumstances may be uncongenial, but they shall not long remain so if you but perceive an ideal and strive to reach it. You cannot travel within and stand still without.

Here is a youth hard pressed by poverty and labour; confined long hours in an unhealthy workshop; unschooled (uneducated), and lacking all the arts of refinement. But he dreams of better things: he thinks of intelligence, of refinement, of grace, of beauty. He conceives of, mentally builds up, an ideal condition of life; the vision of a wider liberty and a larger scope takes possession of him. Unrest urges him to action, and he utilises all his spare time and means, small though they are, to the development of his latent powers and resources.

Very soon, so altered has his mind become that the workshop can no longer hold him. It has become so out of harmony with his mentality that it falls out of his life as a garment is cast aside, and, with the growth of opportunities, which fit the scope of his expanding powers, he passes out of it forever.

Years later, we see this youth as a full-grown man. We find him a master of certain forces of the mind, which he wields with worldwide influence and almost unequalled power. In his hands he holds the cords of gigantic responsibilities; he speaks, and lo! lives are changed; men and women hang upon his words and remould their characters, and, sun-like, he becomes the fixed and luminous centre around which innumerable destinies revolve. He has realised the vision of his youth. He has become one with his ideal.

And you, too, youthful reader, will realise the vision (not the idle wish) of your heart, be it base or beautiful, or a mixture of both, for you will always gravitate towards that which you, secretly, most love. Into your hands will be placed the exact results of your own thoughts; you will receive that which you earn; no more, no less. Whatever your present environment may be, you will fall, remain, or rise with your thoughts, your vision, your ideal. You will become as small as your controlling desire; you will become as great as your dominant aspiration.

## When the Student is Ready, the Master will Appear

In the beautiful words of Stanton Kirkham Davis,

*"You may be keeping accounts, and presently you shall walk out of the door that for so long has seemed to you the barrier of your ideals, and you shall find yourself before an audience—the pen still behind your ear, the ink stains on your fingers—and then and there shall pour out the torrent of your inspiration.*

*You may be driving sheep, and you shall wander to the city—bucolic (naive) and open-mouthed; shall wander under the intrepid guidance of the spirit into the studio of the master, and after a time he shall say, 'I have nothing more to teach you.' And now you have become the master, who did so recently dream of great things while driving sheep. You shall lay down the saw and the plane to take upon yourself the regeneration of the world."*

## There is no Such Thing as Luck

The thoughtless, the ignorant, and the indolent (lazy), seeing only the apparent effects of things and not the things themselves, talk of luck, of fortune, and chance. Seeing a man grow rich, they say, "How lucky he is!" Observing another become intellectual, they exclaim, "How highly favoured he is!" And noting the saintly character and wide influence of another, they remark, "How chance aids him at every turn!"

They do not see the trials and failures and struggles which these men have voluntarily encountered in order to gain their experience; have no knowledge of the sacrifices they have made, of the undaunted efforts they have put forth, of the faith they have exercised, that they might overcome the apparently insurmountable, and realise the vision of their heart.

They do not know the darkness of the heart-aches; they only see the light and joy, and call it "luck". They do not see the long and arduous journey, but only behold the pleasant goal, and call it "good fortune". They do not understand the process, but only perceive the result, and call it "chance".

In all human affairs, there are efforts, and there are results, and the strength of the effort is the measure of the result. Chance is not. Gifts, powers, material, intellectual, and spiritual possessions are the fruits of effort; they are thoughts completed, objects accomplished, visions realised.

The vision that you glorify in your mind, the ideal that you enthrone in your heart—this you will build your life by, and this you will become.

# 7

# SERENITY

*The more tranquil a man becomes,*
*the greater is his success, his influence,*
*his powerfor good...*
*The strong, calm man is always*
*loved and revered.*

# Serenity

Calmness of mind is one of the beautiful jewels of wisdom. It is the result of long and patient effort in self-control. Its presence is an indication of ripened experience, and of a more-than-ordinary knowledge of the laws and operations of thought.

A man becomes calm in the measure that he understands himself as a thought-evolved being, for such knowledge necessitates the understanding of others as the result of thought. And as he develops a right understanding, and sees more and more clearly the internal relations of things by the action of cause and effect, he ceases to fuss and fume and worry and grieve, and remains poised, steadfast, serene.

The calm man, having learned how to govern himself, knows how to adapt himself to others; and they, in turn, revere his spiritual strength, and feel that they can learn of him and rely upon him. The more tranquil a man becomes, the greater is his success, his influence, his power for good. Even the ordinary trader will find his business prosperity increase as he develops a greater self-control and equanimity, for people will always prefer to deal with a man whose demeanour is strongly equable (serene).

The strong, calm man is always loved and revered. He is like a shade-giving tree in a thirsty land, or a sheltering rock in a storm.

"Who does not love a tranquil heart, a sweet-tempered, balanced life?" It does not matter whether it rains or shines, or what changes come to those possessing these blessings, for they are always sweet, serene, and calm.

That exquisite poise of character, which we call serenity is the last lesson of culture; it is the flowering of life, the fruitage of the soul. It is precious as wisdom, more to be desired than gold—yes, than even fine gold. How insignificant mere money seeking looks in comparison with a serene life—a life that dwells in the ocean of truth, beneath the waves, beyond the reach of tempests, in the Eternal Calm!

## Contentment is an Art

How many people we know who sour their lives, who ruin all that is sweet and beautiful by explosive tempers, who destroy their poise of character, and make bad blood! It is a question whether the great majority of people do not ruin their lives and mar their happiness by lack of self-control. How few people we meet in life who are well-balanced, who have that exquisite poise which is characteristics of the finished character!

Yes, humanity surges with uncontrolled passion (anger), is tumultuous with ungoverned grief, is blown about by anxiety and doubt. Only the wise man, only he, whose thoughts are controlled and purified, makes the winds and the storms of the soul obey him.

Tempest-tossed souls, wherever you may be, under whatsoever conditions you may live, know this—In the ocean of life, the isles of Blessedness are smiling, and the sunny shore of your ideal awaits your coming. Keep your hands firmly upon the helm of thought. In the ship of your soul reclines the commanding Master:

He does but sleep: wake Him.

Self-control is strength;

right thought is mastery;

calmness is power.

Say unto your heart, "Peace, be still!"